UNLOCKING THE QUAYSIDE

Newcastle Gateshead's historic waterfront explored

Vanessa Histon

Introduced by Ian Ayris

Tyne Bridge Publishing

Acknowledgements

Tyne Bridge Publishing gratefully acknowledges the assistance of Ian Ayris, Historic Environment Manager for Newcastle City Council; Newcastle Visitor Information Centre; Newcastle Gateshead Initiative; Gateshead Council; Ouseburn Regeneration Team.

Our thanks to Insite Environments, the Landscape and Urban Design Consultants for their generous support. Insite Environments work in a variety of sectors from education and infrastructure through to housing and regeneration projects and are well known for their innovative application of Virtual Reality to visualise development proposals.

Our thanks also to Mott MacDonald for their kind support.

Maps are by Tony Liddell (www.tynescapes.co.uk)

Photography: Sam Fairless, title page, 17, 18, 19, 20, 25, 32, 37, 38, 44, 45, 46, 51, 52, 53, 55, 57, 60, 61, 69, 72, 79, 81, 83; Lynn Pearson, front cover, 21, 75, 82; Harry Bennett, 10; Tony Flowers, 38, 44; Sally Ann Norman 45; Insite Environments 3, 56, 77 (Derek Henderson), 69; Ouseburn Regeneration Team 70, 73 (Lara Baker); Newcastle Gateshead Initiative, 2, 12, 26, 51, 54, 74 (Roger Coulham), 94; Gateshead Libraries 93; other photographs by Anna Flowers. Archive photographs are from the collections of Newcastle Libraries, Local Studies Section.

ISBN: 1 85795 157 3
978 1 85795 157 8

Published by
City of Newcastle upon Tyne
Newcastle Libraries & Information Service
Tyne Bridge Publishing
2006

www.tynebridgepublishing.co.uk

Printed by Elanders Hindson, North Tyneside

Unlocking the Quayside's history 🗝

Like the river itself, the Newcastle Gateshead Quayside never stands still. It has become a spectacular place to see and experience, yet only a few decades ago the look, the atmosphere and even the reputation of the area were quite different.

The transformation began in the 1980s when decaying transit sheds and murky factories were demolished to make way for imposing Law Courts and for the glittering palaces of commerce which now stretch along Newcastle's east Quayside. The pace has not slackened and the ambition not lessened – the arrival of the Gateshead Millennium Bridge, the conversion of the former Baltic Flour Mill and the building of Sage Gateshead have created a stunning physical and cultural environment. This is the modern Quayside, but there have been many others. The history of this short stretch of river is one of continual change.

The east Quayside, above in 1992, and below a similar view in 2005.

Every two or three generations, as if fearful of standing still for too long, man and the elements have imposed themselves on the life and appearance of the riverbank. In 1763 the old Town Wall, which had dominated and protected the Quayside for five centuries, was dismantled. Only eight years later floods swept away the great bridge which had spanned the river since medieval times. With the building of a new bridge across the Tyne an era of change was underway for the medieval town, including a brand new Customs House on the Quayside.

In 1854 the explosive contents of a Gateshead warehouse threw flames across the river, destroying property and taking lives. The Great Fire helped rid the area of many of its ancient cholera-infested houses and alleys. In their place came modern streets and buildings – a transformation which culminated with the replacement of the 18th century stone bridge with Armstrong's marvellous hydraulically powered Swing Bridge – itself a symbol of Victorian Tyneside's ingenuity and industry. A new generation of Tynesiders in a new century extended the quay and spanned the river with the iconic third Tyne Bridge.

A journey along this stretch of the riverbank is also a journey through time. It is the site of a Roman river crossing, in the shadow of a medieval castle, with a matchless collection of historic bridges, some of the region's finest old buildings, and now also the most modern of cultural environments. Its fortunes, like the river, have ebbed and flowed. There has been great innovation – Robert Stephenson's twin-deck High Level Bridge, Armstrong's Swing Bridge, the Co-operative Wholesale Society Warehouse, the extraordinary design of Sage Gateshead – but there has also been poverty and decline and a seamier and darker side. The Milk Market area of the Quayside in Victorian times was 'an unsavoury location … crumbling and decayed'.

The contrasts and variety survive today but thankfully in different ways – in the scale of the buildings and the mix of new and old. The newest buildings on the Newcastle riverside, Trinity Square, share Broad Chare with the some of the oldest – Trinity House.

Baltic – built for milling and storing flour – is now a major national art gallery. The 19th century warehouses of the Milk Market are now apartments. Tynesiders of just 50 years ago would hardly recognise the place.

The thread that runs through the story of the riverside is that of people and trade. Until industry and 'port-life' in general obliged them to look elsewhere, Newcastle Quayside housed many of the town's most important merchants. It then became an area dominated by inns, taverns, boarding (and bawdy) houses and outdoor markets. By the 19th century a huge variety of cargoes and people from many nations regularly thronged the quay. 'There are baskets of fruit and potatoes by the thousand', wrote one historian in 1885, '… hay and moss litter, cheese, butter and eggs, bacon and lard … there is live stock – pigs, loudly protesting and sheep, quiet and gently being driven on shore; while great droves of cattle are hustled and prodded, and beaten and dragged and hurried off to their various destinations.'

A recently restored board on King Street recalls the many destinations of the Tyne Tees Shipping Company.

Today both sides of the river once more throb with activity – visitors, office-workers, people going to pubs, clubs and restaurants, loafers, ramblers and shamblers enjoying the riverside walk, culture-seekers on their way to events. It's a remarkable and fascinating place – but then it always has been.

Ian Ayris, Historic Environment Manager, 2006

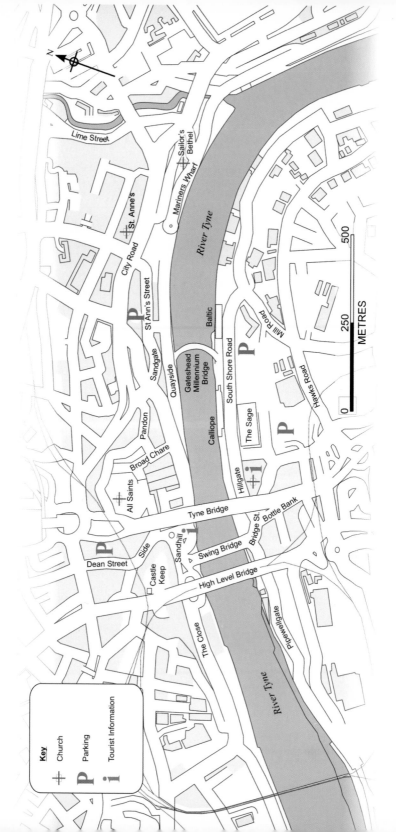

Exploring the riverside

The story of the riverside, and our walk, starts in The Close, one of the oldest parts of Newcastle. The walk gradually leads you forward in time as you wander past medieval warehouses, 17th century merchants' houses, 18th century churches, 19th century shipping offices and 20th century artworks. Crossing the Gateshead Millennium Bridge brings you into to the 21st century and the magnificent, futuristic Sage Gateshead music centre, before you stroll back to the north bank to complete this circular tour.

Looking west along the Tyne during the Tall Ships Race, July 2005.

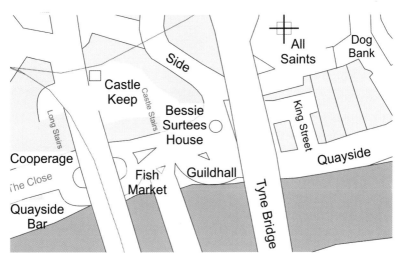

The Close

The Close is an ancient street stretching west from the Swing Bridge. One of Newcastle's oldest thoroughfares, it was probably so named for the simple reason that it was once a very narrow lane. Between the 13th and 15th centuries the townsfolk tipped rubbish into the river here, which became landfill and eventually the solid ground upon which the street is built.

Until the 18th century The Close was home to many of Newcastle's wealthiest residents. Quayside, the restaurant and bar beside the river at No. 35 is probably the oldest surviving timber framed dwelling in Newcastle. It is a good example of a medieval merchant's house with long, narrow warehouses and its own wharf where goods were loaded and unloaded.

Quay Fact

From 1691 until 1835, Newcastle's Mansion House stood on the Close. As well as the Mayor's home, it was the venue for sumptuous dinners and elaborate balls. When the Quayside became more run down, the Mansion House was relocated to a better part of town. The old building was used as a warehouse until it was destroyed by fire in 1895.

The Cooperage pub on the opposite side of the Close at Nos. 32-34 dates from the 15th century. According to a local story its wooden frame was recycled from the timbers of a ship which sank in the Tyne. Because the building backs onto a steep slope there was no room to extend it, so when the owners needed

The Quayside Bar, 35 The Close.

more space they simply added a new storey using bricks brought over from Holland as ships' ballast. The Cooperage was extended in this way every hundred years or so.

By the middle of the 18th century the more prosperous residents of The Close began to move to quieter (and cleaner) parts of the town, away from the river. Warehouses and small industries, including a flour mill and glass, iron and soap works, took their place.

Quay Fact

The Cooperage takes its name from the cooper, or barrel maker, who moved his business into the building in the 19th century. Barrel making was an extremely important trade in the days when all kinds of goods, including fish, vinegar and fruit, as well as beer and wine, were transported and stored in barrels. The photographs on page 63 (and opposite) give an idea of the number of barrels regularly arriving at or leaving the Quayside.

*Barrels a-plenty in the yard of the Queens Head Hotel, 39 The Close,
on 8 September 1907.*

Sandhill around 1890, with the Guildhall on the left.

The wonderfully timbered Bessie Surtees House is above J W Newton & Co. Look for the opaque glass pane in the first floor window from which Bessie is said to have eloped. The house is preserved by English Heritage.

Castle Stairs climb steeply between the old houses to the Castle Keep and give a fascinating view of the rear of these buildings.

Sandhill

The Sandhill is so called because it was once just 'a Hill of naked Sand, when the tide was out. For formerly the Tyne overflowed all this Place ... it is a spacious Place and adorned with buildings very high and stately, whose Rooms speak the Ancient Grandeur, being very large and Magnificent.'

You can still see some of the houses that were so described by Henry Bourne, writing in in 1736. Dating from the 16th and 17th centuries, some have their original facades, while others were later remodelled with Georgian frontages. If you have the time (and the stamina) you can climb nearby Castle Stairs to see the backs of these fascinating old houses.

Sandhill was once the place to buy fish, herbs, bread, cloth, leather and other goods, as well as a place for public gatherings. Proclamations were made here and people flocked to see bull baiting and bonfires, plays and public executions.

The Lort Burn flows beneath Newcastle, to an outfall into the Tyne at Sandhill. An art work, *Tributary* by John Maine, celebrates this now hidden stream on the Side and at Sandhill.

A view from Sandhill towards the warehouses of The Close, c.1900.

Quay Fact

No. 41 Sandhill, which dates back to the 16th century, was once the home of wealthy banker Aubone Surtees and the setting for Newcastle's favourite love story. Aubone's daughter, Bessie, fell in love with John Scott, a coal trader's son, who was born in Love Lane, a little further along the Quayside. Surtees disapproved of the match, so one night in 1772, Bessie climbed out of the window of the house to elope with her lover. Aubone had been wrong about Scott, who had an extremely successful political career, eventually becoming Lord Eldon, Chancellor of England. He and Bessie had a long and happy marriage.

Bessie Surtees House peeps between the Watergate and the Guildhall.

The Guildhall

The Guildhall was built by Robert Trollope in the 1655 to replace an earlier building. The classical front we see today was added in the late 18th and early 19th centuries. It was once the administrative centre of the town and housed the offices of the Corporation, the Merchant Adventurers' Court and Court of Assize. It contains court fittings dating from the late 18th and early 19th centuries, including a fearsome spiked dock. Part of the ground floor is now a Visitor Information Centre.

Watergate Building, designed by John Dobson, is just west of the Guildhall. A hidden treasure still lies under the road here, accessed from the Watergate cellars: a ribbed arch from the medieval Tyne Bridge which was destroyed by catastrophic flooding in 1771.

Quay Fact

The columns at the east end of the Guildhall once surrounded the fish market, built by Newcastle's well-known architect John Dobson in 1823. At first the fishwives really disliked the building and Dobson was very unpopular. The women soon realised, however, that compared to selling fish in all weathers from their old stalls dotted around the windy Quayside, the new market was warm and comfortable. As a peace offering, they selected some choice fish which they took to Dobson's house on Christmas day. In 1880 a new fish market was built to the west of the Swing Bridge. Though it now houses a night club, the river god Tyne, Neptune and two fishwives still look down on passers-by to remind us of the past. The old fish market was enclosed and became a news room.

Neptune, standing on two fat fish, flanked by severe-looking fishwives gazes imperiously down from the Fish Market of 1880.

Tyne Bridges

Beside Watergate Building is the Swing Bridge; a very important bridge in Tyneside's history but by no means the first to stand on this site. The first known bridge at Newcastle was the Roman Pons Aelius which was built around 122AD, roughly on the site of the present Swing Bridge. It probably had a wooden deck which rested on stone piers. Stone altars, dedicated to the gods Oceanus and Neptune, were found on the river bed during the 19th century; these had probably been set up by the Roman Sixth Legion to protect Pons Aelius.

We don't know much about river crossings between Newcastle and Gateshead from the early 5th century, when the Romans withdrew from Britain, until the end of the 12th century. We do know that in 1248 a new stone bridge was built, on the line of the old Roman Bridge, to replace a predecessor which had been destroyed by fire. It must have been a splendid structure with pointed stone arches, and towers (one of which was used as

Seven bridges span the Tyne between Newcastle and Gateshead today. It was not always so. For many centuries the only crossing was a narrow bridge on the site of today's Swing Bridge.

a prison), shops, houses and at least one chapel built on it. From 1698 the bridge carried the pipes which brought Newcastle's water supply from Gateshead. The medieval bridge was swept away by severe floods in November 1771.

A detail from Buck's drawing of Newcastle made in 1745 and showing the old bridge. The medieval Maison Dieu (hospice) and Guildhall are on the Quayside to the right of the picture. The Town Wall stretched along the Quayside as far as Sandgate to the east.

The collapse of the medieval bridge brought severe difficulties for Newcastle and Gateshead. However, within ten days of the disaster a free ferry service was running between the two towns, and by 22 October 1772, a temporary bridge was opened. Three years later, work on a permanent stone bridge, on the line of the medieval bridge was well underway. It opened in April 1781.

The Swing Bridge

As technology advanced and the type of vessels using the Tyne began to change, the Georgian stone bridge caused problems for river traffic. The bridge's low arches blocked the passage of even medium-sized ships. This meant, for example, that coal for export had to be brought downstream in small flat bottomed boats called keels and loaded into ships waiting below the bridge. The arrangement did not suit William George Armstrong, a local entrepreneur, whose engineering works up river at Elswick were unable to expand because of the difficulties of transporting raw materials and finished goods. His company produced an innovative replacement bridge which had sophisticated machinery allowing it to swing open for ships to pass through.

This photograph, dating from 1863, taken from St Mary's Church, Gateshead, shows how the Georgian Tyne Bridge of 1781 presented an obstacle to traffic. Immediately below the photographer is the area devastated by the fire and explosion of 1854 (see page 29). All the buildings are blackened by years of pollution. The Tyne was less busy by this time than it had been before Newcastle quay was extended eastwards to Sandgate – once boats would have been tied up in the river five or six deep. Just by the Guildhall was still the mooring point for the weekly steamer service to Aberdeen.

The temporary bridge in 1871, the piers of the old bridge still visible.

The Georgian Tyne Bridge was demolished and a temporary bridge was built to carry traffic while the new one was under construction. The Swing Bridge was completed in 1876 and at the time was the largest swing bridge ever built. The hydraulic mechanism which opens the bridge was converted from steam to electric power in 1959, but otherwise most of the original design features are still in working order today. Perhaps because of that, the Swing Bridge, is probably the most important hydraulic turning bridge in the UK, or even the world. It is still manned 24 hours a day, 365 days a year.

The Swing Bridge, still in good working order today.

The High Level Bridge

A little way up river of the Swing Bridge is the High Level Bridge, designed by the great engineer, Robert Stephenson, to carry both road and rail traffic. The first passenger train to cross the bridge left Newcastle at 9.30am on 15 August 1849. The High level was official opened on 28 August that year, when Queen Victoria's train stopped on the bridge on a return journey from Scotland. The Queen did not leave the train, but listened to an address which was read to her while she and the Prince Consort 'surveyed with the greatest possible interest, the magnificent scene around and below them'.

Quay Fact

The roadway of the High Level Bridge was popular with Tyneside's gamblers. In 1859 a journalist from a local newspaper reported that because it is a quarter of a mile of long, straight, covered track and could be closed off at both ends it made an ideal track for dog racing.

A pristine High Level Bridge in 1864.

The Great Fire of 1854

The High Level Bridge has often been used as a grandstand for events on the river such as races and regattas. Spectators also used it to view one of the most dramatic events in Tyneside's history. It all started shortly after midnight on 6 October 1854 when a fire broke out in a textile mill in Hillgate, Gateshead. News of the blaze spread quickly and thousands of people lined the bridges and the quays to watch firemen, soldiers and volunteers struggle to control the flames. The fire soon threatened neighbouring buildings. Suddenly, at 3.10 am, there was a series of terrifying explosions which were heard as far away as Hartlepool. The heat had ignited chemicals stored in an adjacent warehouse. Blazing sulphur, stones, bricks and burning timbers were hurled across the river and straight into the crowds of spectators on the north bank. The explosion killed over 50 people and many of the densely-packed buildings on the Newcastle side began to burn. Their old, dry timbers ignited quickly and soon the fire raged on both sides of the river. Fire engines and soldiers were brought in from as far away as Berwick and Carlisle, but it was nightfall before they managed to get the blaze under control.

The conflagration destroyed many of Newcastle's and Gateshead's oldest buildings and made hundreds of people homeless. Some good did come out of the tragedy, however. The buildings that were consumed by the fire included many of the most derelict and insanitary in the two towns. Elegant new buildings replaced the alleys destroyed on the on the north side of the river. Many originally housed the offices of shipping companies; you can still see how grand they are and get some idea from their elegance of 19th century Newcastle's importance as a port.

Quay Fact

John Dobson was the architect for much of the redevelopment of Newcastle Quayside after the fire. Ironically his son, Alexander, also an architect, was trying to help put out the fire in Gateshead when the chemical warehouse exploded. As buildings collapsed, tons of burning debris fell into the narrow street, killing Alexander and several others. He was only 26. It is intriguing to wonder whether John Dobson saw the work he did in rebuilding the Quayside as a monument to the son he lost.

The wreckage on the Quayside on the morning of 7 October 1854.

A survivor of the fire sandwiched between Victorian buildings, 1964.

The Quayside, 2005.

Tyne Bridge

Probably the best-known of Newcastle's bridges, The Tyne Bridge has been a potent symbol of Tyneside ever since it was opened by King George V on 10 October 1928. Its 162 metre span was built in two halves, advancing from opposite banks of the river, and it is a tribute to the skill and precision of the engineers and workers that they eventually met in the middle. The new bridge was painted with green paint, specially developed by a Gateshead company, and the colour was faithfully reproduced when it was repainted in 2000. The walls on the Gateshead side

of the bridge were faced with stone reclaimed from the demolition of Carliol Street gaol in Newcastle. Giant Cornish granite towers stand at each end of the bridge. They were designed as warehouses and contained lifts to transport passengers and goods to the Quayside. The warehouses were never used – ironically, the Tyne Bridge gave quick and easy access to the upper part of Newcastle so the Quayside became less important to the city's commercial life.

Quay Fact

Many people believe that the Tyne Bridge was the prototype for the Sydney Harbour Bridge, but in fact the Australian bridge was commissioned first. Both bridges were built by the same company, Dorman, Long of Middlesbrough. Ralph Freeman, the designer of the Sydney Harbour Bridge, was consulting engineer on the Tyne Bridge. Work began in Sydney in January 1925, and on Tyneside in August of the same year, although the Tyne Bridge, being much shorter and narrower, was completed more than three years before its Australian cousin.

The Tyne Bridge and bustling Quayside in 1928, the year of its opening.

Dorman Long commissioned a series of progress photographs.

Here the final diagonal of the bracing is positioned, 23 February 1928.

All Saints Church 🗝

From the bottom of King Street there is a spectacular view of the elliptical All Saint's Church (now St Willibrord with All Saints), designed by David Stephenson and consecrated in 1796. The consecration was celebrated in a fairly unorthodox manner when John Burdikin, a soldier in the Cheshire Militia, climbed to the top of the steeple (a dizzying 195 feet above the ground) and did a handstand. According to contemporary reports he held the position for some time. His reasons for doing this are lost to history, but a taste for dangerous stunts obviously ran in the family. In 1816, when the steeple needed repairing, Burdikin's son was the bricklayer who was given the job. While he was working on the repairs he took the opportunity to recreate his father's escapade.

Quay Fact

In 1858 the beadle of All Saints church hit on a grisly way of supplementing his income. At dead of night he would steal down to the churchyard, open a grave and take the lead lining from the coffin. Although people in neighbouring houses noticed the flickering light from the lantern he used, they assumed that it was caused by ghostly activity and kept well away. Soon, however, the beadle was selling suspicious amounts of lead. Some brave souls kept watch in the churchyard overnight and caught him red-handed (or possibly lead-handed!).

Quayside buildings 🗝

There are some fine old buildings on the Newcastle bank of the river; for a splendid panorama look down from the viewing platform of Baltic.

Many of the buildings formed part of the redevelopment of the Quayside after the great fire. One is Exchange Buildings, a large stone office block designed by William Parnell in the early 1860s. Equally impressive offices, such as Mercantile Building

All Saints Church from the Quayside. Visit the church and churchyard by climbing the stairs at the end of King Street.

(built in 1883 by J C Parsons) at Nos. 15-23 were erected later in the 19th century. John Wardle built Nos. 25 and 27 as a shop and offices in 1869.

At No. 31 is Three Indian Kings House. A pub called The Kings occupied this site; the current name dates from at least 1735. Three Indian Kings is thought to refer to the three wise men in the nativity story.

The Customs House at No. 39 was built at the centre of the Quayside in 1766. In the 1830s it was refronted to a design by Sidney Smirke. When the Tyne was packed with trading ships the Customs House was the centre for the collection of duty on imports such as tea, spices or rum.

The Customs House, left in 1965, and right, more recently after cleaning. Above the door is the Hanoverian Royal Coat of Arms.

The smoke-blackened but elegant Victorian buildings and the traditional Sunday Market (which still takes place weekly) around 1920.

This 1830 map gives us a picture of the Quayside around 180 years ago.
The Mansion House, already run down and about to be abandoned, is
on the riverside at The Close. Opposite, on the other side of the Close,
is the Town Wall. The Wall is also seen further east, protecting the
Quay itself. Sets of stairs along the Close climb up to the Castle.

The Georgian Tyne Bridge, its Blue Stone marking the boundary
between Newcastle and County Durham, is the only crossing. The
dotted line of the Lort Burn can be seen snaking down through
Sandhill past the fish market. To the east of the Guildhall (Exchange)

the narrow lanes or chares of the medieval town stretch back towards All Saints. Conditions were crowded and the wooden warehouses and tenements would become ready tinder for the fire that was to wreck the Quayside 24 years later.

On the Gateshead side there is far less building except for the crowded conditions of Pipewellgate and Hillgate to the west and the east of the bridge. It was a fire at Wilson's worsted mill in Hillgate that started the 1854 fire. St Mary's Church, now Gateshead Visitor Centre, has watched over the changing river scene for around 900 years.

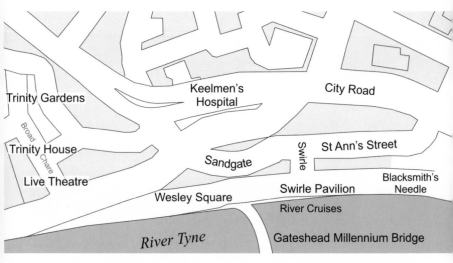

The central Quayside. Between Wesley Square and the Swirle Pavilion are Sandgate Steps, the Malmaison Hotel, Keelman Square and the Pitcher and Piano.

The Chares

Before the great fire, Newcastle's Quayside was criss-crossed with dark, narrow alleys know as chares (apparently derived from the Anglo-Saxon world *cerre*, meaning a turning). They had evocative names such as Dark Chare, Peppercorn Chare, Armourer's Chare and Blue Anchor Chare. Another chare, Love Lane, was once the home of Bessie Surtees' sweetheart, John Scott. Although the chares had once been home to many of Newcastle's richest and most influential citizens, by the early 19th century they were insanitary and insalubrious. Historian Eneas Mackenzie, writing in 1827, commented that Plummer Chare was 'the receptacle of Cyprian Nymphs whose blandishments were of the most coarse and vulgar description. Indeed most of these dark lanes were inhabited by very dangerous though not very tempting females'.

According to Mackenzie, Broad Chare was unusual because it 'is broad enough to admit a cart. Most of the old houses have been pulled down and lofty commodious warehouses erected in their place. A narrow flagged foot path runs up the west side, but it is neither a safe nor a pleasant place.'

Quay Fact

If you are brave enough to walk along Broad Chare late at night you may hear the rustling of a woman's dress and a soft chuckle. You may even see a veiled figure beckoning you to approach. Be very afraid, because if you do you'll find that the mysterious woman has no head. She is said to be the ghost of Martha Wilson, a seaman's widow who, suffering from depression, hanged herself in her room in the almshouses of Trinity House in 1817.

Trinity Chare, Broad Chare and Spicer Lane open onto the Quayside, 1895. The building housing Chadburn's Telegraph Company would soon make way for Baltic Chambers.

Live Theatre, Broad Chare. Note the old warehouse windows.

Broad Chare and Trinity Gardens

Some of the warehouse space described by Mackenzie is now occupied by Live Theatre. The theatre has commissioned work from some of the North East's finest playwrights, including Alan Plater, C P Taylor, Julia Darling and Lee Hall (the script for the film Billy Elliot had early readings here); it also encourages new talent. As well as collaborating with the Royal Shakespeare Company on special projects, the Live has close associations with actors such as Tim Healy and Robson Green.

Further up Broad Chare is Trinity House, home of the

Guild of Masters and Mariners. This powerful guild administered river traffic, collected dues, provided lighthouses and trained river pilots. Some of the buildings around the courtyard date from the early 16th century and others were added during the late 18th century. They include a rigging loft, a banqueting hall and almshouses as well as a chapel. The chapel window, which can be seen from Broad Chare, dates from 1794.

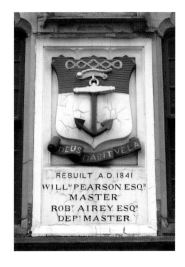

At the top of Broad Chare lie Trinity Gardens with a focal-point sculpture, *Give and Take*.

Carved from a 36-tonne glacial boulder, which was unearthed near Fort William in Scotland, *Give and Take* is sited metres above one of Newcastle's hidden rivers, the Pandon Burn. Sculptor Peter Randall-Page used the naturally eroded shape of the boulder and carved the surface with 630 hexagons and 12 pentagons – a pattern found in many natural, molecular and atomic structures.

The result is an artwork produced by both man and the elements. The sculpture stands on a cobbled surface representing a dry riverbed, which was created by Randall-Page to acknowledge the Pandon Burn still flowing beneath the city's streets.

Newcastle Law Courts.

On the east side of Broad Chare are the Law Courts which opened in 1990. The unusual pink sandstone, not found in the North East, was chosen to complement the surrounding red brick buildings. The porthole-shaped windows are a tribute to the maritime traditions of the Quayside.

Sandgate Markets

The milk market was the place, just beside the site of the present-day Law Courts, where townsfolk bought milk, butter, cheese and other country produce. It was also the site of the 'hirings' where agricultural workers came to find work with local farmers. A butcher market was held every day. There has been a milk market on the Quayside since at least 1717. The name suggests a clean, wholesome place, filled with pretty dairymaids and handsome countrymen, but the reality, as described by an observer in 1881, was very different.

'It was an unsavoury locality, haggling and bargaining over the wretched rags going on all day long between the shabby

Hunting for a bargain outside Ripley's general store around 1900.

Barefoot children and squalid conditions at the Milk Market public water fountain around 1890. A street musician provides an attraction.

buyers and the shabbier sellers ... The crumbling decayed old buildings that look as though they only waited for a moderate gust of wind to convert them into a site of rubbish, form a fitting background to a picture such as only Dickens could ever paint.'

The writer was most likely referring to Paddy's Market, a second- (third- and fourth-) hand clothes market, held on Saturdays on the Milk Market site until the mid 20th century. Originally clothes were hung about the old town walls or heaped on piles of straw in the street. It was probably called Paddy's Market because of the large Irish population living in the surrounding densely-packed and semi-derelict alleys. In 1851 around one third of the people living in Sandgate were born in Ireland; they generally had unskilled, poorly paid occupations, hence their need for cheap second-hand clothing.

Making the Milk Market even less wholesome was the Sandgate midden, a vile rubbish dump where the town scavenger emptied carts full of street sweepings, slaughter house waste and other unpleasant substances. Today's environmental health officers would be appalled at its proximity to a place selling food. From time to time the contents of the midden were sold for manure and taken away by keelboat or farmer's cart.

Warehouses (now converted into apartments) tower over Sandgate children around 1900. They seem cheerful in spite of bare feet and ragged clothes. Many of them may have been the children of Irish immigrants who arrived on Tyneside to escape the famine and disease following the potato blight of the 1840s. The fathers of these children probably worked at the nearby docks.

The Pitcher and Piano's architecture reflects the river's history. The sandstone wall represents a ship's hull and the frontage echoes the scaffolding used in the Tyne shipyards.

Sandgate took its name from the gate in the old town wall, which stood (not surprisingly) on the sand here. Many of its former residents worked in jobs directly connected with the river. They included shipwrights, mariners and keelmen. The keelmen rowed coal and other goods up and down river in flat-bottomed keelboats – essential for negotiating the low arches of the old Tyne Bridge. Skilled craftsmen, such as joiners, cabinet makers and smiths, lived here too. These groups tended not to live in the same streets as the Irish community, but even so conditions were dirty and overcrowded. Much of the slum housing in this area was demolished by the beginning of the 20th century.

Quay Fact

The pink granite obelisk in Wesley Square is the Wesley Memorial, erected in the Milk Market 1891 to mark the centenary of the death of John Wesley, the founder of Methodism. Wesley and his brother Charles often visited Newcastle to preach and to give pastoral care to prisoners in the gaol. In 1742, John Wesley preached in Sandgate which he described as 'the poorest and most contemptible part of town'. The fountain was moved to its present site during Quayside redevelopment.

Art around Sandgate

The wall by the Wesley Memorial follows the line of the old town wall which was demolished in 1763. Built in sandstone, the wall was carved on site by Neil Talbot in 1996. The relief, called *River Tyne*, shows

a map of the Tyne with views of places along the river's length. The Lighthouse is one of three illuminated features (the others are at Sandgate Steps) by Cate Watkinson.

Siren (1995) and *River God* (1996) are bronze partner sculptures by Andre Wallace. *River God* holds a staff and chain and looks as though he is blowing at

Siren, who wears a bell for an earring.

Keel Row (1996) was inspired by the famous Tyneside song, *Weel may the Keel Row*, which originated in the 18th century.

Neil Talbot carved the scenes, including, of course, a keelboat, which are taken from engravings by T H Hair in *A Series of Views of the Collieries of Northumberland and Durham* (1841). Graciela Ainsworth incised the words of the song. The iron-work railings, handrails and lamp columns were designed by Alan Dawson.

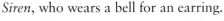

Quay Fact

If you climb Sandgate Steps you will see the clock tower of the Keelmen's Hospital. The working life of a keelman was difficult, strenuous and dangerous and there were many accidents. The Keelmen's hospital opened in 1701 to care for sick and injured keelmen and the widows and orphans of keelmen. It was funded by contributions from the keelmen themselves.

Baltic, the River God, and Gateshead Millennium Bridge from Sandgate Steps.

Art in Keelman Square

The two sculptures in Keelman Square were made by Andrew Burton in 1996.

Column and Steps consists of a series of curving forms, which could be read as waves, surrounding a tapering column. The column has a gear-like capital topped by a twisting abstract shape. Many of the shapes used in the sculpture, as well as the iron of its construction, reflect the Tyne's industrial heritage.

Rudder is a huge bronze rudder-like form, taking its inspiration from the vessels that sailed to and from the Tyne.

Left, the Quayside and the CWS Warehouse in the 1970s.
Above, the transformation is complete.

Quay Fact

The Malmaison hotel (named after the home of Josephine, wife of Napoleon Bonaparte) was built between 1897 and 1900 as a warehouse for the Co-operative Wholesale Society. Constructed from concrete reinforced with iron, one of the most modern building materials of the day, the warehouse has a concrete exterior which is finished to look like Portland stone. Now transformed, it is now probably the oldest surviving large-scale ferro-concrete building in the country.

The Swirle

The oddly-named Swirle probably takes its name from the now hidden Swirle or Squirrel burn which runs into the Tyne here. It once marked the boundary between Newcastle and the separate town of Byker. According to R J Charleton, writing in 1885, here 'sat the Sandgate lasses in their tubs amongst the shallow water near the edge, washing tripe and singing old Newcastle ditties.'

The Swirle Pavilion is half sculpture, half folly. Made by Raf Fulcher in 1998, the names of some of the cities with which Newcastle traded are carved around the inner rim.

Behind the Swirle Pavilion is Half Moon Square, named after an inn which stood nearby. The inn is commemorated by a stone half moon in the centre of the square.

Half Moon Square, St Ann's Wharf and the Swirle Pavilion.

Surrounding Half Moon Square is St Ann's Wharf, an office development. Named for the classical church of St Anne (but with a variant spelling), which stands on the hill behind it and to the east, this was once the sailing point for ships to Antwerp, Hamburg and Rotterdam. One of the office suites is occupied by engineers Mott Macdonald. As Mott Hay and Anderson they designed both the Tyne Bridge and the Redheugh Bridge. More recent work includes the Sage just across the river.

The Swirle in 1926. The general provisions shop, J and S Bruce, below the Colman's Mustard sign, had been in the Bruce family since 1847.

The Blacksmith's Needle

This conical sculpture, 7.6metres tall, was created in 1996 by members of the British Association of Blacksmith Artists to a design by Alan Dawson. Each of the six tiers represents one of the senses, including the mysterious sixth sense. Each tier contains objects relating to its particular sense as well as sea creatures and other items with a maritime theme. In 1997, percussionist Evelyn Glennie inaugurated the work by ringing the bell which hangs inside the needle.

Work, wharves, warehouses and cargoes

You are now in an area which used to be known as North Shore and was the heart of the Quayside's industrial area and transport systems.

Proximity to the river made this an ideal place to set up a business as the cost of transporting goods and raw materials would be hugely reduced. During Quayside redevelopment in the 1990s the demolition of a warehouse near the Malmaison hotel revealed the remains of lime kilns thought to date from the 14th century. Quayside industries included soap making, brewing, brush making and metal forging. Many trades were directly connected with shipping; chain, anchor and ships' lamp manufacture, for example. On the North Shore itself were several early shipyards; Hopper's Yard, Fulton's Yard, Hopper's Slipway and Wright's Yard. There was a ropery as well as ship's chandlers, block and mast makers, carvers and painters.

It is hard to imagine now, but the Tyne was once crowded with ships. Until the middle of the 19th century these were sailing ships, their tall masts and rigging filling the sky. In the second

The masts of sailing ships still dominate this Sunday Market scene near the Customs House in 1900.

The Quayside east of Milk Market in 1908, with merchandise covering the wharf.

A similar view in 2005.

Aberdeen Wharf, just by the Guildhall, 19 November, 1912.

half of the century they were gradually replaced by steam ships. All were loading and unloading cargoes at the many wharves along the river. The wharves were named after the destinations of the ships that berthed there: Aberdeen; Hull; Leith; London; Hamburg; Rotterdam; Antwerp; and Malmo. The wharves had

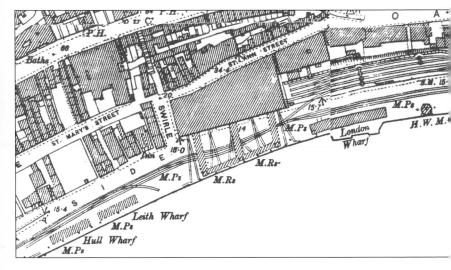

spouts for transferring grain and coal directly into the ships' holds – one, known as the Dandy Gears, had three spouts to load coal into three ships at once. There were numerous cranes for loading and unloading everything from food to engines.

Of course these goods had to be transported to and from the Quayside. Horse and cart was the usual method until the 19th century and the advent of rail. In 1842 the Victoria tunnel was opened. It carried an underground railway which ran for over two miles under Newcastle's busy streets, transporting coal from Spital Tongues colliery to the river. As the colliery closed in 1857 the railway had a short life, but the tunnel that carried it is still there. In 1870 another Quayside railway opened. This linked the Tyne with Manors station. Building the railway (and indeed driving the locomotives) was a difficult task because of the steep gradient up the river valley, but the line remained open until 1969.

It was also important to have warehouses to store the goods that came through the port. At first these were adapted from existing Quayside buildings, particularly those in the narrow chares. During the 19th and early 20th centuries, however, huge purpose-built warehouses were constructed, often following the lines of the Quayside's medieval alleyways. A large group of the warehouses built in the first 30 years of the 19th century used stone recycled from the old town wall. Some of them are still in use as apartments.

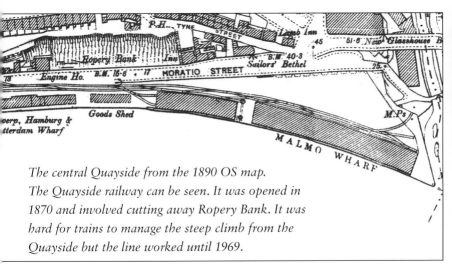

The central Quayside from the 1890 OS map. The Quayside railway can be seen. It was opened in 1870 and involved cutting away Ropery Bank. It was hard for trains to manage the steep climb from the Quayside but the line worked until 1969.

Volvo car bodies are loaded for shipment to Sweden, 1965.

Antwerp, Hamburg and Rotterdam Wharf, 1913.

What were the cargoes that passed through Newcastle? The Tyne's most important export was coal. In 1830, for example, 11,226 colliers left the Tyne carrying over two million tons of coal. In the same year only 148 vessels sailed out with other cargoes. Other exports included coke, tar, grindstones, chemicals and manufactured goods. The ships would return carrying an enormous range of commodities: timber (used for pit props) from the Baltic; citrus fruits from the Mediterranean; sulphur, lead and iron ore; grain, butter salt and livestock. Even the ballast brought back by the ships was used. The glass and ceramic industries of the Ouseburn valley grew up because the sand, limestone, clay and flint they needed were carried into the Tyne as ballast on colliers.

Tyne ships also carried human cargoes. Every week Scandinavian emigrants arrived in Newcastle *en route* for America. Regular ferry services took passengers to ports such as Aberdeen, London, Trondheim, Oslo and Bergen. Even in the mid 20th century it was still possible for people travelling to London and other British ports to take a berth on a ship rather than make the journey by road or rail.

At this point in your walk you can choose to cross the Tyne by Gateshead Millennium Bridge (see page 74). Alternatively continue walking upriver on the Newcastle bank to the flats on Mariner's Wharf. Behind the flats is a slim, grey spire belonging to the Sailor's Bethel, which opened in 1875 as a non-conformist church with a resident missionary. Perhaps the sailors were less interested in their souls than in the various distractions of the Quayside's many pubs, because the Bethel has had many uses over the years. As well as a church for Danish seamen, it has been a community centre and a doll's hospital. Since 1992 it has been head office of Insite Environments, the landscape and urban design company which has made a major contribution to Quayside regeneration.

Quay Fact

The Sailor's Bethel caught the eye of artist L S Lowry. His 1965 oil painting of the building is in Newcastle's Laing Art Gallery.

The Sailor's Bethel, bottom right in the photograph, looks a little lonely in the midst of massive Quayside regeneration, 1995.

The Sailor's Bethel. The rather fine gargoyle is possibly one of the last gargoyles to grace a building in Newcastle.

At present this modest but unique Victorian church is an appropriate home for the head office of Insite Environments.

Ouseburn

At the end of Mariner's Wharf is the steel and glass sculpture *Confluence*, made in 1999 by Sue Woolhouse and Jim Roberts. Two steel panels are linked by a forged metal fish, representing the coming together of two rivers (the Ouseburn and the Tyne).

The name Ouseburn is thought to be derived from 'Ewes Burn', and although it sounds like a tranquil rural spot, it was once one of the most heavily industrialised sections of the riverside. Writing in 1827, Eneas Mackenzie described the area as: 'A Plebeian district covered with extensive and important manufactories consisting of corn steam mills, foundries, potteries, a flaxmill and other works.' By 1885 conditions seem to have worsened and R J Charlton writes: 'We find it, black and sullen, flowing among the most forbidding surroundings ...'

Today, if you explore inland, you will find a transformed valley nestling below spectacular bridges with pubs, cafes artists' studios and attractions such as Ouseburn Farm, Stepney Bank Stables and Seven Stories, the Centre for Children's books.

Now retrace your steps west and cross the Tyne by Gateshead Millennium Bridge.

Quay Fact

Glassmaking began in the Ouseburn in about 1619 with the building of three glasshouses. Thirty years later, local historian William Grey commented that 'upon the north side of the river is Ewes Burne, over which is a wooden bridge, which goeth down to a place called the Glass-Houses, where plaine glasse for windowes are made, which serveth most parts of the Kingdom.'

Above, the Ouseburn Valley in 2005, Glasshouse Bridge far right.

Below, the mouth of the Ouseburn in 1906. The old bridge came down in 1908, but the pub (the Tyne) is still there below Glasshouse Bridge.

Gateshead Millennium Bridge

Gateshead Millennium Bridge, the world's first tilting bridge, opened to the public on 17 September 2001 and was officially opened by the Queen in May 2002. It was hailed as a 'beautiful structure' by experts and by the millions of people worldwide who had watched (on television, on the Internet, and from the banks of the Tyne) as the massive bridge was brought upriver from Wallsend on the giant crane Asian Hercules II, and lowered carefully into place. The other Tyne bridges are for trains and heavy transport. This quieter crossing is for walkers and cyclists only and links to the Hadrian's Way Cycle Path.

> **Quay Fact**
>
> This elegant bridge, designed by architects Wilkinson Eyre, has won numerous awards including the Royal Institute of British Architects Stirling Prize in 2002. Geordies are rightly proud of their new icon.

Containing enough steel to make 64 double-decker buses, the whole structure pivots, like an eye slowly opening, when ships need to pass under the arch. Each opening and closing takes around 4 minutes. A computer-controlled lighting system ensures that the bridge looks equally spectacular at night.

Above, the illuminated arch.

Left, the Gateshead Millennium Bridge shows off its tilt during the 2005 Tall Ships visit.

Weighing over 800 tonnes, Gateshead Millennium Bridge rests on concrete foundations which extend 30 metres down, anchoring it to the riverbed. It is 126 metres long and the top of the elegant arch curves 50 metres above the river (unless it is tilting of course). The grey posts in the river are to guide shipping through the deepest channel.

Next to Baltic is Baltic Quay, a residential development of flats and penthouse suites. In only a few years this area has been totally transformed as you will see from the following pages. Take a few moments to enjoy the bridge, take in the banks of the Tyne on both sides and the vista of bridges to the west.

Photographed from a similar spot to the one on the previous page, this photograph shows the Baltic Flour Mill during the 1950s.

Baltic

On the south side of the Millennium Bridge is Baltic the Centre for Contemporary Art. Opened in 2002, the centre has several galleries, as well as studio, performance and cinema/lecture space, making it one of the largest contemporary art spaces in Europe. The building also incorporates viewing areas giving stunning panoramas of the Tyne.

As well as offering a stimulating programme of exhibitions, Baltic has hosted residencies by internationally famous artists including Anthony Gormley and Spencer Tunick who have worked with local people to create major art projects.

Quay Fact

Baltic is housed in a former grain warehouse and flour mill. It was owned by Rank and opened in 1949. All the Rank mills were named after seas and Baltic, of course, is no exception.

Tucked beneath the silvery curves of the Sage, and flying the White Ensign, is the 'stone frigate' HMS Calliope.

HMS Calliope

On the river bank to the west of Baltic is HMS *Calliope*, not a ship at all but a 'stone frigate', the North East's Royal Naval Reserve Training Centre. There has been a Royal Naval Reserve Division on the Tyne since 1905. The original HMS *Calliope* was a real ship that arrived in the Tyne in 1907 and was used as a drill ship. She was moored near the Vickers Armstrong works at Elswick, where she stayed until she was broken up in 1951. Her replacement, *Falmouth*, was renamed *Calliope*. She served at Elswick until 1968, when the Division moved to its present shore-based training centre in Gateshead. There are plans to develop and improve the site between Baltic and the Sage and along the river frontage here. A refurbishment of HMS *Calliope* may form part of these developments.

> ### Quay Fact
>
> The eastern section of HMS *Calliope* is a former pipe works. The western section was a parcel sorting office until 1987 when it was converted to extend the training centre.

The Sage Gateshead

The Sage Gateshead opened in December 2004 as a regional centre for music and musical discovery. With three performance spaces, it hosts concerts ranging from classical music to folk, rock, jazz and blues, as well as providing innovative musical education for people of all ages.

The Sage was designed by architects Foster & Partners. Each auditorium was built as a separate enclosure. The gigantic, shell-like roof which covers and contains the halls consists of 3,000 stainless steel panels and 250 glass panels. The foyer provides magnificent views across the Tyne.

Walk through the foyer of the Sage to St Mary's Square and you will see St Mary's Church ahead of you.

The Sage comes into its own at night when its lights are reflected in the Tyne, and the view from inside, of the river and bridges, is stunning.

Hall One of the Sage dominates the interior. The enormous panes of glass have to be washed by abseiling window cleaners.

In contrast with the colourful photographs on the previous pages, this view of Gateshead shows the town in 1924, before the Tyne Bridge was built. Traffic is held up because the Swing Bridge is open, and horses and carts and cars are backed up Bridge Street and Bottle Bank.

A rowing race on the Tyne around 1860 shows the crowded homes and industry just west of the High Level Bridge.

By 1854 there were proposals to build a Corporation Quay at Hillgate, on the east side of the present Swing Bridge, which it was hoped would totally transform 'one of the dirtiest and most unwholesome places in the kingdom'. The developers had useful and timely assistance from the great fire which destroyed most of Hillgate later that year. The Quay was built, but it lacked facilities and could never compete with its neighbour across the river. By the 1920s businesses were leaving the riverside and during the 1930s the slums were cleared away. In 1929 and 1930 large sections of the Quay fell into the river, and though it was repaired it never prospered.

Quay Fact

During the 19th century rowing was the Tyne's favourite sport, sometimes attracting eager crowds of 50,000-100,000. The Tyne produced several star rowers including Harry Clasper from Dunston, Robert Chambers from Newcastle and Gateshead's James Renforth who won World Championships in 1868 and 1870. There is still an annual regatta on the Tyne.

As industry on the Tyne declined during the 1970s and 1980s, Gateshead Quayside fell into disrepair. However, the whole area is now undergoing massive regeneration.

St Mary's Church

Built between the 12th and 14th centuries (with a tower rebuilt in 1740), St Mary's church was the only Anglican church in Gateshead until 1825. Until the late 18th century all baptisms in the town were performed here. It was the only place where people could be married before 1825 or buried before 1811. Although for centuries it was the centre of life in the town, it was severely damaged by the fire of 1854 and again in 1979. It lay empty for some years and was deconsecrated. At present Gateshead Visitor Centre is situated there.

Quay Fact

In 1080 St Mary's was the scene of a violent clash between the ruling Normans and the native Saxons. Walcher, the Norman Bishop of Durham, was suspected of being involved in the murder of a Saxon – these were tense times. Walcher and his men were attacked by a mob in Gateshead and took refuge in an earlier church near this site. The mob then set fire to the building. As the Normans escaped from the blazing church, they were murdered one by one. The occupying Normans could not allow this affront and the following uprising to go unpunished so in reprisal William's half-brother Odo, Bishop of Bayeux, laid waste to all the land between Tees and Tweed.

Top, St Mary's today.

Below, St Mary's above the houses of Hillgate from a panorama painted (with some artistic licence) by James Storey around 1870.

Left, St Mary's and Gateshead in the 1890s.

Gateshead Quay on 18 May 1928, shortly before the Tyne Bridge was completed. The bridge towers were still under construction.

At this time the Quay was leased to the Tyne Tees Steam Shipping Company. Part of the Quay would collapse within two years.

Follow the road either along South Shore Road from the north side of St Mary's or down hill from St Mary's Square towards the Swing Bridge. Whichever way you approach the bridge you will pass a sculpture by David Pearl, Gateway Beacon 1 (Gateway Beacon 2 is on Eastgate). The six-metre high stainless steel and translucent blue column is at the foot of Bridge Street.

As you reach the Swing Bridge you will notice the entrance to Pipewellgate to your left. This narrow street is one of the historic streets of Gateshead (others include Hillgate, Bridge Street, Bottle Bank, High Street, and Oakwellgate).

Gateway Beacon 1 by David Pearl.

Quay Fact

Bottle Bank, which leads down to Bridge Street, is one of the the oldest streets in Gateshead. During excavations for the building of the Hilton Hotel, archaeologists discovered evidence of a Roman road and buildings. You might assume that the name Bottle Bank refers to the glassworks that operated on the Gateshead shore, but in fact it is derived from the Saxon word 'botl', meaning a house or dwelling.

The River Tyne Police Gateshead divisional headquarters in 1970. Opened in 1911, and shared with the harbour authorities, it was refurbished in 1983. The main police station was at South Shields.

The smart restaurant overlooking the Tyne on the corner was a headquarters of the River Tyne Police from 1911 to the early 1990s. The River Tyne Police were established in 1845 (the earliest such force in the world) to keep thieves away from the ships and warehouses. The 20 policemen, who patrolled the wharves, jetties and quays of the Tyne, looking for thieves and other villains, were at first armed with cutlasses and used rowing boats (they acquired a steam-powered launch in 1900). An earlier police station and 'dead house' (mortuary) were at Ouseburn. Today the Marine Division of Northumbria Police patrol the Tyne and Wear in motor boats and are based at South Shields.

Pipewellgate leads to a sculpture park overlooking the Tyne where you can see works by artists including Andy Goldsworthy and Colin Rose.

Now cross the Swing Bridge to return to Newcastle. The walk ends at the Guildhall. If this tour has encouraged you to find out more about the history, heritage and culture of Newcastle and Gateshead, call in at the Visitor Information Centre and tea rooms located here. You will find information about historic

Rolling Moon by Colin Rose.

buildings, museums and galleries, entertainment and shopping, as well as advice on accommodation and transport.

The Guildhall from the Swing Bridge.
Right, some traffic you probably won't see today. Sandhill around 1930.

Further information

Newcastle Visitor Information is located at the Riverside entrance, Guildhall, Quayside, and at 132 Grainger Street, Newcastle upon Tyne.
Telephone: 0191 2778000
Fax: 0191 2778009
email: tourist.info@newcastle.gov.uk

www.newcastle.gov.uk

Gateshead Visitor Information is located at St Mary's Church, Oakwellgate, Gateshead.
Telephone: 0191 4784222
Fax: 0191 4785380
email: tourism@gateshead.gov.uk

www.gateshead-quays.com

www.visitnNewcastleGateshead.com

Further reading

Find out more about Newcastle Gateshead Quays in the following books available from Tyne Bridge Publishing:

Crossing the Tyne, Frank Manders and Richard Potts
Lost Shipyards of the Tyne, Dick Keys and Ken Smith
Tall Ships on the Tyne, Dick Keys and Ken Smith
Bygone Quayside and the Chares, Jack and John Leslie
Bygone West Quayside and the Close, Jack and John Leslie
James Renforth of Gateshead, Ian Whitehead

www.tynebridgepublishing.co.uk